THE SUMMER OLYMPIC GAMES

PERCY LEED

LERNER PUBLICATIONS ◆ MINNEAPOLIS

Copyright © 2025 by Lerner Publishing Group, Inc.

Statistics in this book are accurate through the 2020 Summer Olympic Games.

All rights reserved. International copyright secured. No part of this book may be reproduced, stored in a retrieval system, or transmitted in any form or by any means—electronic, mechanical, photocopying, recording, or otherwise—without the prior written permission of Lerner Publishing Group, Inc., except for the inclusion of brief quotations in an acknowledged review.

Lerner Publications Company
An imprint of Lerner Publishing Group, Inc.
241 First Avenue North
Minneapolis, MN 55401 USA

For reading levels and more information, look up this title at www.lernerbooks.com.

Main body text set in Mikado.
Typeface provided by HVD Fonts.

Photo Editor: Nicole Berglund
Lerner team: Sue Marquis

Library of Congress Cataloging-in-Publication Data

Names: Leed, Percy, 1968- author.
Title: The summer Olympic games / Percy Leed.
Description: Minneapolis, MN : Lerner Publications, [2025] | Series: Lerner sports rookie. Championship games | Includes bibliographical references and index. | Audience: Ages 5–8 | Audience: Grades K–1 | Summary: "Every four years, the world's best athletes compete in the Summer Olympics. Learn about the history, great moments and athletes, and vibrant cultures of the Summer Games"— Provided by publisher.
Identifiers: LCCN 2024012926 (print) | LCCN 2024012927 (ebook) | ISBN 9798765648025 (library binding) | ISBN 9798765661536 (paperback) | ISBN 9798765653999 (epub)
Subjects: LCSH: Olympics—Juvenile literature.
Classification: LCC GV721.53 .L44 2025 (print) | LCC GV721.53 (ebook) | DDC 796.48—dc23/eng/20240404

LC record available at https://lccn.loc.gov/2024012926
LC ebook record available at https://lccn.loc.gov/2024012927

Manufactured in the United States of America
2-1013110-53363-8/12/2025

TABLE OF CONTENTS

CHAPTER 1
THE SUMMER GAMES ... 4

CHAPTER 2
GREATEST MOMENTS ... 8

CHAPTER 3
BEST ATHLETES ... 12

CHAPTER 4
OLYMPIC FUN ... 18

THE CHAMPS ... 22
FUN FACTS ... 23
GLOSSARY ... 24
LEARN MORE ... 24
INDEX ... 24

CHAPTER 1
THE SUMMER GAMES

Brittney Griner shot the basketball. *Swish!* She scored two points for Team USA!

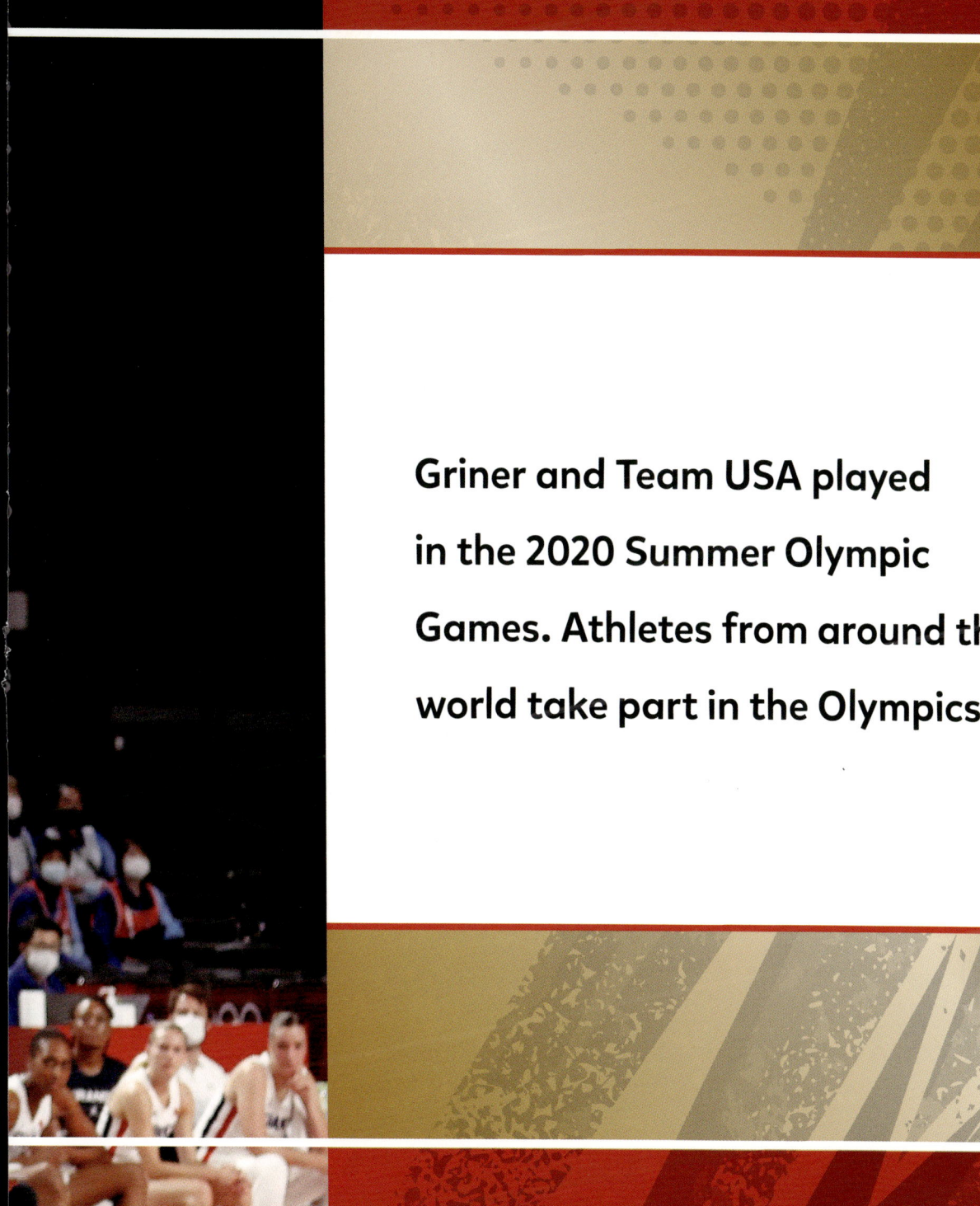

Griner and Team USA played in the 2020 Summer Olympic Games. Athletes from around the world take part in the Olympics.

The first Olympics were in Greece more than 1,000 years ago. Then no Olympics were held for many years. They started again in 1896.

Olympic athletes play for their countries.

CHAPTER 2
GREATEST MOMENTS

Nadia Comaneci was a gymnast at the 1976 Summer Olympics. She scored the first perfect 10!

In 2016, Katie Ledecky won five gold medals in swimming. No one came close to beating her.

Elaine Thompson-Herah won two footraces at the 2016 and 2020 Olympics. She was the fastest woman in the world.

Mutaz Barshim and Gianmarco Tamberi were tied in the high jump in 2020. They chose to share the gold medal.

Gianmarco Tamberi

Mutaz Barshim

Chapter 3
Best Athletes

The US women's basketball team has won nine gold medals.

Steve Redgrave was the greatest rower ever. He won gold at five Summer Olympics.

Steve Redgrave

Michael Phelps won 28 Olympic swimming medals. No one has ever won more medals.

Allyson Felix won more Olympic medals than any other US track-and-field athlete.

Usain Bolt was the fastest man in the world for many years. No one could beat him at three Summer Olympics.

Simone Biles is a superstar gymnast. Many people think she is the best gymnast ever.

CHAPTER 4
OLYMPIC FUN

The Summer Olympics usually takes place every four years. Fans love to watch the athletes in action.

Athletes stay at the Olympic Village. They rest and get ready.

The start and end of the Summer Olympics are big events. People dance and cheer. Fans can't wait for the next Summer Olympics!

THE CHAMPS

Which country won the most medals at the last 10 Summer Games? Keep reading to find out!

Year	Country	Medals Won
2020	United States	113
2016	United States	121
2012	United States	104
2008	United States	112
2004	United States	101
2000	United States	97
1996	United States	101
1992	Unified Team (the former Soviet Union)	112
1988	Soviet Union	132
1984	United States	174

FUN FACTS

Until 1920, gold medals were solid gold. Since then, the medals are only gold on the outside.

Artists such as painters used to compete in the Olympics.

The first Winter Olympics took place in 1924.

GLOSSARY

gymnast: an athlete who jumps, flips, and spins

high jump: a jump over a high bar

rower: an athlete who rows a boat

LEARN MORE

Bolte, Mari. *Gymnastics*. Mankato, MN: Creative Education, 2024.

Gish, Ashley. *Athletics*. Mankato, MN: Creative Education, 2024.

Peters, Katie. *Being a Good Teammate*. Minneapolis: Lerner Publications, 2022.

INDEX

Greece, 6

gymnast, 8, 17

medals, 9, 11–12, 14–15

Olympic Village, 19

swimming, 9, 14

PHOTO ACKNOWLEDGMENTS

Image credits: Ann-Dee Lamour/CDP MEDIA/DPPI/Alamy, p. 4; History and Art Collection/Alamy, p. 6; AP Photo/David J. Phillip, pp. 7, 10, 14; AP Photo, p. 8; AP Photo/Michael Spomer/Cal Sport Media, p. 9; AP Photo/Francisco Seco, p. 11; Robert Gauthier/Los Angeles Times/Getty Images, p. 12; AP Photo/Ruth Fremson, p. 13; AP Photo/Martin Meissner, p. 15; AP Photo/KYDPL KYODO, p. 16; AP Photo/Jeff Roberson, p. 17; Richard Ellis/UPI/Alamy, p. 18; AP Photo/Vladimir Pesnya/Sputnik, p. 19; AP Photo/Loic Baratoux/Abaca/Sipa USA, p. 21. Design element: Winner Creative/Shutterstock. Cover: AP Photo/Kyodo News.